A 52-WEEK COUPLES DEVOTIONAL

Growing in Grace and Love

DOUGLAS ASANTE

**A 52-WEEK COUPLES DEVOTIONAL
GROWING IN GRACE AND LOVE**

Copyright © 2024 by Douglas Asante

All rights reserved. No portion of this book may be reproduced, stored in a retrieval system, or transmitted in any form or by any means - electronic, mechanical, photocopy, recording, scanning, or other - except for brief quotations in critical reviews or articles, without the prior written permission of the publisher.

ISBN: 978-1-916692-19-0

Email the author via **info@dasante.org.uk**
Visit website for more info **www.dasante.org.uk**

Unless otherwise indicated, quotations are taken from the New International Version (NIV)

Published in the United Kingdom by
Equip Publishing House

INTRODUCTION

Marriage is one of God's most beautiful gifts—a sacred bond that reflects His love for His people. Yet, like any journey, marriage comes with its challenges, joys, and seasons of growth. It requires intentionality, grace, and a foundation firmly rooted in Christ. A 52-Week Couples Devotional: Growing in Grace and Love is designed to help you and your spouse strengthen your relationship with God and with one another, one week at a time.

This devotional isn't just about reading Scripture together and living it out. Over the next year, you'll explore key biblical principles that shape a thriving marriage—love, forgiveness, trust, unity, and faithfulness. Each week, you'll walk through a simple structure designed to guide meaningful conversations and foster spiritual intimacy:

* **BIBLE VERSE**: Start with God's Word as the foundation for reflection.

* **OBSERVATION**: Uncover the core truth of the passage.

* **INTERPRETATION**: Explore what it means for your marriage and how it applies to your life.

* **CORRELATION**: Connect the theme to other Scriptures, gaining a fuller perspective of God's wisdom.

* **REFLECTION**: Ask meaningful questions to deepen your understanding and bond.

* **CHALLENGE**: Take actionable steps to apply God's truth in your daily life as a couple.

* **PRAYER**: End by inviting God into your journey, trusting Him to lead and transform your marriage.

Whether you've been married for decades or are just beginning your life together, this devotional is for you. It's an opportunity to grow in grace and love, learning to see each other as God sees you—imperfect but redeemed, flawed yet chosen.

As you embark on this journey, remember that transformation doesn't happen overnight. Some weeks may stretch you, while others will affirm and encourage you. Be patient with one another and, most importantly, with yourselves. Lean into God's grace, and let His love shape your hearts and marriage.

So grab your Bibles, set aside some quiet time together, and let God guide your hearts through His Word. May this devotional be more than just a weekly routine—it's a chance to nurture a love that lasts a lifetime, rooted in the One who first loved us.

Let's grow in grace and love together.

In His love,

D. K. Asante

WEEK 1

1

Building a Foundation of Love

"Unless the Lord builds the house, those who build it labor in vain."

PSALM 127:1 (ESV)

OBSERVATION

This verse highlights the necessity of involving God in every aspect of life, especially in building relationships and homes. Without His guidance, our efforts may feel empty or fail to yield lasting joy.

INTERPRETATION

Marriage, like a house, requires a strong foundation. When we invite God into our relationship, He becomes the cornerstone that ensures stability, growth, and endurance. This verse reminds couples that while their efforts are important, relying on God ultimately gives their union purpose and strength.

CORRELATION

 Jesus emphasised building on a strong foundation in Matthew 7:24-27, comparing a wise person who builds on rock with a foolish one who builds on sand. Couples who prioritise God's presence in their marriage create a sturdy structure, able to withstand life's storms.

REFLECTION

* How often do you actively invite God into the daily workings of your marriage?
* Are you aligning your priorities with His design for your relationship?

CHALLENGE

 This week, set aside time to pray together as a couple, specifically asking God to guide your decisions and strengthen your foundation. Write down one area of your marriage where you want to lean on Him more intentionally.

PRAYER

Heavenly Father, we acknowledge that we cannot build a strong and lasting relationship without You. Help us to make You the centre of our marriage. Teach us to rely on Your wisdom, trust in Your timing, and love each other as You love us. Bless our union so that it may glorify You. In Jesus' name, Amen.

WEEK 2

Love is Patient, Love is Kind

*"Love is patient, love is kind.
It does not envy, it does not boast,
it is not proud."*

1 CORINTHIANS 13:4 (NIV)

OBSERVATION

 This verse defines the essence of love in action. It reminds us that love is not about fleeting feelings but is demonstrated through patience, kindness, humility, and selflessness.

INTERPRETATION

 In a marriage, patience and kindness are essential ingredients for a thriving relationship. These qualities enable couples to navigate challenges and celebrate victories with grace and compassion. When love is devoid of envy or pride, it fosters a secure and supportive partnership.

CORRELATION

Ephesians 4:2-3 encourages believers to *"be completely humble and gentle; be patient, bearing with one another in love."* *This aligns with 1 Corinthians 13:4, showing that love must be lived out daily, especially in our closest relationships.*

REFLECTION

* In what ways do you show patience and kindness to each other?
* Are there moments where pride or envy have hindered your ability to love fully?

CHALLENGE

Choose one way to intentionally practice kindness toward your spouse this week. It could be through a thoughtful gesture, a kind word, or being patient in a situation that might normally frustrate you. Please write it down and reflect on how this act affected your relationship.

PRAYER

Lord, thank You for Your perfect example of love. Teach us to embody patience and kindness in our marriage. Help us to set aside envy, pride, and selfishness so we can love each other as You intended. May our actions reflect Your grace and goodness. In Jesus' name, Amen.

WEEK 3

Forgiveness in Marriage

*"Be kind and compassionate to
one another, forgiving each other,
just as in Christ God forgave you."*
EPHESIANS 4:32 (NIV)

OBSERVATION

 Forgiveness is not just a gift we give others; it reflects the forgiveness God has granted us. This verse calls us to practice kindness and compassion to live out our faith.

INTERPRETATION

 Marriage is a union of two imperfect people, and conflicts are inevitable. Forgiveness is crucial to restoring harmony and strengthening the bond between spouses. By extending grace to one another, we reflect Christ's love and build a resilient relationship.

CORRELATION

Matthew 18:21-22 recounts Peter asking Jesus how many times he should forgive someone, and Jesus replies, "Not seven times, but seventy-seven times." This illustrates the boundless nature of forgiveness, which is necessary for a healthy marriage.

REFLECTION

* Are there unresolved hurts or offences you need to forgive each other for?
* How can you cultivate a spirit of compassion when misunderstandings arise?

CHALLENGE

Identify one area where you've been holding onto resentment. Write it down, pray about it, and have an honest, loving conversation with your spouse about moving forward in forgiveness.

PRAYER

Heavenly Father, thank You for forgiving us even when we fall short. Please help us to extend that same forgiveness to one another. Heal our hearts where there is hurt, and give us the courage to let go of grudges. May we grow in compassion and unity as we follow Your example. In Jesus' name, Amen.

WEEK 4

4

Honoring Each Other

*"Be devoted to one another in love.
Honor one another above yourselves."*

ROMANS 12:10 (NIV)

OBSERVATION

 This verse emphasises selflessness in relationships, urging believers to love and honour each other wholeheartedly. True devotion prioritises the well-being and dignity of the other person.

INTERPRETATION

 Honouring your spouse means valuing their needs, feelings, and contributions. It's about lifting each other with words and actions, creating an environment of mutual respect and affirmation.

CORRELATION

 Philippians 2:3-4 encourages us to "do nothing out of selfish ambition or vain conceit. Rather, in humility, value others above yourselves." Honouring our spouse is a practical application of this biblical principle.

REFLECTION

* Do your actions and words reflect honour and devotion to one another?
* How can we make honouring our spouse a daily practice?

CHALLENGE

 Take time this week to affirm your spouse. Write them a note of appreciation or express gratitude for something they've done recently. Observe how this small act of honour strengthens your bond.

PRAYER

Lord, help us to honour each other as You have honoured us with Your love and sacrifice. Teach us to be devoted, selfless, and encouraging in our marriage. May our words and actions build each other up and reflect Your goodness. In Jesus' name, Amen.

WEEK 5

5

Communication that Builds Up

*"Let no corrupting talk come out
of your mouths, but only such as is good
for building up, as fits the occasion,
that it may give grace to those who hear."*

EPHESIANS 4:29 (ESV)

OBSERVATION

 This verse reminds us of the power of words. What we say can either build up or tear down those around us. Grace-filled communication strengthens relationships and reflects God's love.

INTERPRETATION

 In marriage, words have the ability to nurture intimacy or create distance. Speaking with kindness, thoughtfulness, and grace fosters understanding and unity. Couples are called to use their words to encourage and uplift each other.

CORRELATION

Proverbs 18:21 says, "The tongue has the power of life and death." This reinforces the importance of choosing words wisely, especially when communicating with your spouse during times of conflict or stress.

REFLECTION

* Do your conversations with each other reflect grace and encouragement?
* How can you improve our communication to ensure it builds trust and connection?

CHALLENGE

This week, practice active listening with your spouse. Set aside time to discuss a topic important to them without interrupting or offering solutions unless asked. Affirm what they've shared and thank them for opening up.

PRAYER

Lord, thank You for the gift of communication. Teach us to use our words to build each other up and not to tear down. Please help us to listen with open hearts and speak with grace, kindness, and wisdom. May our conversations reflect Your love. In Jesus' name, Amen.

WEEK 6

6

Trusting God in Times of Uncertainty

*"Trust in the Lord with all your heart,
and do not lean on your own understanding.
In all your ways acknowledge him,
and he will make straight your paths."*

PROVERBS 3:5-6 (ESV)

OBSERVATION

 This passage calls for complete trust in God, especially during times of uncertainty. It reminds us that His plans are greater than ours and that He is always faithful to guide us.

INTERPRETATION

 In marriage, challenges and uncertainties are inevitable. Trusting God together strengthens the bond between spouses. It shifts the focus from personal worries to God's promises, fostering unity and hope.

CORRELATION

 Psalm 37:5 says, "Commit your way to the Lord; trust in him, and he will act." This reinforces the importance of surrendering our plans and anxieties to God, allowing Him to lead us as a couple.

REFLECTION

* Are there areas in your life or marriage where you struggle to trust God?
* How can you encourage each other to lean on Him during times of uncertainty?

CHALLENGE

 Identify one area of uncertainty in your life as a couple. Spend time in prayer together, surrendering that specific issue to God and trusting Him to provide clarity and peace.

PRAYER

Father, thank You for Your faithfulness and wisdom. Teach us to trust You with all our hearts, especially when we face uncertainty. Help us to lean on Your understanding, not our own, and guide us as we navigate life together. In Jesus' name, Amen.

WEEK 7

7

Serving Each Other in Love

*"For even the Son of Man came
not to be served but to serve,
and to give his life as a ransom for many."*

MARK 10:45 (ESV)

OBSERVATION

This verse shows Jesus as the ultimate example of servant-hearted love. His willingness to serve others, even to the point of sacrifice, is the standard for how we should treat one another.

INTERPRETATION

Marriage thrives when both spouses adopt an attitude of service toward one another. Serving in love means putting your spouse's needs above your own and finding joy in caring for them as Christ cares for the Church.

CORRELATION

 Galatians 5:13 encourages believers to "serve one another humbly in love." This principle applies powerfully in marriage, where humble service strengthens the bond between spouses and reflects God's love for the world.

REFLECTION

* In what ways do you currently serve each other?
* Are there areas where you can be more intentional in meeting one another's needs?

CHALLENGE

 Perform an act of service for your spouse this week that goes beyond your usual routine. Whether it's taking on one of their responsibilities or doing something unexpected, let your actions demonstrate love and care.

PRAYER

Lord, thank You for showing us what it means to serve in love. Help us to follow Your example in our marriage, seeking ways to care for and support one another selflessly. May our acts of service bring us closer together and glorify You. In Jesus' name, Amen.

WEEK 8

The Power of Unity

*"Though one may be overpowered,
two can defend themselves. A cord of three
strands is not quickly broken."*

ECCLESIASTES 4:12 (NIV)

OBSERVATION

 This verse emphasises the strength that comes from unity, especially when God is at the centre of a relationship. Together, a couple can face challenges more effectively than they can alone.

INTERPRETATION

 A strong marriage is built on teamwork and mutual support. When couples rely on each other and invite God into their union, they create a resilient bond against life's difficulties.

CORRELATION

Jesus prayed for unity in John 17:21, saying, "That all of them may be one, Father, just as you are in me and I am in you." Unity in marriage reflects God's design and serves as a testimony of His love.

REFLECTION

* How do you prioritise unity in your relationship?

Are there areas where you feel divided, and how can you address them together?

CHALLENGE

This week, identify one goal or project you can work on together as a couple. Whether it's a home task, financial plan, or spiritual practice, use it as an opportunity to strengthen your teamwork and unity.

PRAYER

Father, thank You for the gift of unity in marriage. Help us to stand together in love, supporting and encouraging each other in every situation. May You always be the third strand in our relationship, giving us strength and wisdom. In Jesus' name, Amen.

WEEK 9

Walking in Humility

"Do nothing out of selfish ambition or vain conceit. Rather, in humility value others above yourselves."

PHILIPPIANS 2:3 (NIV)

OBSERVATION

 This verse teaches the importance of humility in relationships. It challenges us to put others' needs before our own, fostering an attitude of love and selflessness.

INTERPRETATION

 Humility is essential in marriage. When both spouses prioritise each other's well-being, conflicts are reduced, and love grows. Humility involves listening, forgiving, and acknowledging when we're wrong. It reflects Christ's attitude and strengthens the bond between husband and wife.

CORRELATION

Colossians 3:12 reminds believers to "clothe yourselves with compassion, kindness, humility, gentleness, and patience." These qualities create a harmonious and loving relationship, especially within marriage.

REFLECTION

* How can you show humility in your marriage this week?
* Are there times when pride has prevented you from resolving conflicts or expressing love?

CHALLENGE

This week, practice humility by letting go of one personal preference in favour of your spouse's desire. Reflect on how this act of selflessness brings peace and unity to your relationship.

PRAYER

Lord, thank You for the example of humility You set through Jesus. Teach us to approach each other with humility and love. Please help us to let go of pride and serve one another selflessly. May our marriage glorify You. In Jesus' name, Amen.

WEEK 10

Embracing Gratitude in Marriage

*"Give thanks in all circumstances;
for this is the will of God
in Christ Jesus for you."*

1 THESSALONIANS 5:18 (ESV)

OBSERVATION

 This verse encourages believers to maintain an attitude of gratitude regardless of circumstances. Gratitude shifts our focus from problems to blessings, allowing us to see God's goodness in every situation.

INTERPRETATION

 Taking each other for granted or focusing on imperfections is easy in marriage. Practising gratitude helps us recognise and appreciate the positive aspects of our spouse and relationship, cultivating a heart of contentment and joy.

CORRELATION

Colossians 3:15 reminds us to "let the peace of Christ rule in your hearts...and be thankful." Gratitude brings peace to a marriage and creates a stronger connection between spouses.

REFLECTION

* Do you take time to express gratitude for one another?
* How can focusing on thankfulness transform your outlook on our relationship?

CHALLENGE

Every day this week, take a moment to express one thing you're thankful for about your spouse. Write it down, say it aloud, or share it in prayer together. Reflect on how this practice strengthens your connection.

PRAYER

Father, thank You for the gift of marriage and the blessings we experience each day. Teach us to embrace gratitude in all circumstances. Help us to see the good in each other and celebrate Your goodness in our lives. In Jesus' name, Amen.

WEEK 11

Overcoming Fear Together

*"There is no fear in love,
but perfect love drives out fear."*

1 JOHN 4:18 (NIV)

OBSERVATION

 This verse highlights the power of God's perfect love to cast out fear. Fear can disrupt relationships, but love brings peace and confidence when rooted in God.

INTERPRETATION

 Fear of failure, rejection, or uncertainty can create tension in marriage. God's love equips couples to face these fears with courage and faith. Couples can foster a sense of safety and reassurance in their relationship by leaning on His promises.

CORRELATION

 Isaiah 41:10 says, "Do not fear, for I am with you." This promise reminds us that God's presence is our ultimate source of courage, especially during trials.

REFLECTION

- Are there fears or anxieties affecting your relationship?
- How can you support each other in trusting God when you feel afraid?

CHALLENGE

 This week, share one fear or anxiety you've been carrying with your spouse. Pray together about it, asking God to replace fear with His perfect love and peace.

PRAYER

Heavenly Father, thank You for Your perfect love that casts out fear. Teach us to trust in Your promises and lean on each other during times of uncertainty. Please help us to replace fear with faith as we walk this journey together. In Jesus' name, Amen.

WEEK 12

Rejoicing in Each Other

"Rejoice in the wife of your youth."
PROVERBS 5:18 (NIV)

OBSERVATION

This verse calls couples to find joy in their marriage and celebrate one another as a gift from God. Rejoicing in your spouse strengthens love and rekindles passion.

INTERPRETATION

Over time, the responsibilities and routines of life can overshadow the joy of marriage. This verse reminds couples to intentionally cultivate delight and gratitude for each other, keeping their love vibrant and joyful.

CORRELATION

 Ecclesiastes 9:9 says, "Enjoy life with your wife, whom you love." God desires for couples to cherish and celebrate their relationship, reflecting His joy and love for His people.

REFLECTION

* How can you rekindle joy and excitement in your relationship?
* Are you taking time to celebrate the gift of your marriage?

CHALLENGE

 Plan a special date or activity this week to celebrate your marriage. Whether it's a dinner, walk, or simply reminiscing together, use the time to reflect on the blessings of your relationship.

PRAYER

Lord, thank You for the gift of my spouse and the joy they bring into my life. Please help us to cherish and celebrate each other daily. May our marriage reflect Your love and bring glory to Your name. In Jesus' name, Amen.

WEEK 13

13

The Strength of Commitment

"What therefore God has joined together, let not man separate."

MARK 10:9 (ESV)

OBSERVATION

 This verse emphasises the sacred nature of marriage, reminding us that it is God who joins a couple together. It's a covenant that requires steadfast commitment and unity.

INTERPRETATION

 Marriage is not just a contract but a spiritual covenant before God. It involves a lifelong promise to love, honour, and support each other through every season. When couples remember the divine foundation of their union, they can better navigate challenges with perseverance and faith.

CORRELATION

Ecclesiastes 5:4-5 reminds us, "When you make a vow to God, do not delay in fulfilling it." This reinforces the seriousness of marriage vows and the importance of honouring them as an act of worship.

REFLECTION

* Do we view our marriage as a covenant or just a commitment?
* How can we honour the sacredness of our union in our daily interactions?

CHALLENGE

This week, renew your commitment to each other in a tangible way. Write down or verbally express what you promise to continue doing for your spouse, such as loving them in tough times or prioritising their needs.

PRAYER

Lord, thank You for joining us together in marriage. Please help us to honour this sacred bond and remain faithful to our vows. Give us the strength to persevere through challenges and the wisdom to seek You in all things. In Jesus' name, Amen.

WEEK 14

The Gift of Peace

*"Blessed are the peacemakers,
for they shall be called sons of God."*
MATTHEW 5:9 (ESV)

OBSERVATION

 Jesus calls His followers to be peacemakers, reflecting God's character by fostering reconciliation and harmony in their relationships.

INTERPRETATION

 In marriage, being a peacemaker means choosing understanding over argument, forgiveness over bitterness, and love over pride. Peace doesn't mean avoiding conflict but resolving it in a way that strengthens your bond and honours God.

CORRELATION

 Romans 12:18 says, "If possible, so far as it depends on you, live peaceably with all." This principle applies directly to marriage, encouraging couples to pursue peace even when it requires sacrifice.

REFLECTION

* Do you approach conflict with the goal of peace and reconciliation?
* How can you be more intentional about creating an environment of peace in your home?

CHALLENGE

 The next time a disagreement arises, pause and pray together before continuing the discussion. Commit to speaking with gentleness and listening with an open heart. Reflect afterwards on how this approach changed the outcome.

PRAYER

Father, thank You for being the ultimate source of peace. Help us to bring Your peace into our marriage by seeking understanding and reconciliation. Teach us to handle conflicts with grace and love, reflecting Your character. In Jesus' name, Amen.

WEEK 15

Cultivating Joy in Daily Life

"The joy of the Lord is your strength."
NEHEMIAH 8:10 (NIV)

OBSERVATION

 This verse reminds us that true joy comes from the Lord and is a source of strength during good times and difficult seasons.

INTERPRETATION

 In marriage, joy is more than fleeting happiness—it is a deep and abiding confidence in God's faithfulness. Couples who find joy in the Lord can face challenges with resilience and gratitude, and their shared joy becomes a testimony of God's goodness.

CORRELATION

 Psalm 16:11 says, "You make known to me the path of life; in your presence there is fullness of joy." This reinforces the idea that joy is found in a relationship with God, which in turn strengthens relationships with others.

REFLECTION

* How can you cultivate joy together in your daily routines?
* Are you finding strength in the joy of the Lord during challenging times?

CHALLENGE

 Each day this week, take turns sharing one moment of joy you experienced, no matter how small. End the day by thanking God for these blessings together.

PRAYER

Lord, thank You for being the source of our joy and strength. Help us see Your blessings in our lives and find joy every season. May our marriage reflect the joy that comes from knowing You. In Jesus' name, Amen.

WEEK 16

Living Generously

*"Each of you should give what you have
decided in your heart to give,
not reluctantly or under compulsion,
for God loves a cheerful giver."*

2 CORINTHIANS 9:7 (NIV)

OBSERVATION

 This verse speaks to the importance of giving with a joyful heart. Generosity is about material gifts and giving time, love, and care freely to others.

INTERPRETATION

 In marriage, generosity means going beyond what is expected to serve and love your spouse. It also involves being generous together as a couple, using your blessings to support and encourage others. Generosity reflects God's abundant love and deepens your connection with each other.

CORRELATION

Proverbs 11:25 says, "A generous person will prosper; whoever refreshes others will be refreshed." This principle applies to marriage, as acts of generosity refresh and bless the relationship.

REFLECTION

* Are you generous in giving time, attention, and love to each other?

* How can you use your marriage to bless each other generously?

CHALLENGE

Find one way to bless your spouse this week through an act of generosity. Additionally, as a couple, identify a way you can give to someone in need, whether through time, encouragement, or resources.

PRAYER

Lord, thank You for the generosity You've shown us through Your love and provision. Teach us to be generous with our time, love, and resources, both with each other and with those around us. May our marriage be a reflection of Your abundant grace. In Jesus' name, Amen.

WEEK 17

17

Forgiving as Christ Forgives

"Be kind and compassionate to one another, forgiving each other, just as in Christ God forgave you."
EPHESIANS 4:32 (NIV)

OBSERVATION

 This verse highlights the importance of forgiveness in relationships, reminding us that Christ's example sets the standard. Forgiveness is a gift we give, reflecting God's grace.

INTERPRETATION

 In marriage, offences are inevitable, but harbouring resentment can create barriers to intimacy. Choosing to forgive as Christ forgives fosters healing, reconciliation, and growth. Forgiveness is an act of love that breaks the cycle of bitterness and opens the door for restoration.

CORRELATION

 Colossians 3:13 also says, "Bear with each other and forgive one another if any of you has a grievance against someone. Forgive as the Lord forgave you." This reinforces the call to show the same grace we've received from God.

REFLECTION

* Are there unresolved hurts in your relationship that need forgiveness?

* How can you actively practice forgiveness in your daily interactions?

CHALLENGE

 This week, take time to reflect on any lingering grievances. Share these with your spouse in a loving and respectful way, then pray together for healing and commit to forgiving one another fully.

PRAYER

Lord, thank You for the forgiveness we receive through Christ. Please help us to extend the same grace to each other, letting go of past hurts and building a stronger bond. May forgiveness bring peace and unity to our marriage. In Jesus' name, Amen.

WEEK 18

Patience in Every Season

"Be completely humble and gentle; be patient, bearing with one another in love."

EPHESIANS 4:2 (NIV)

Observation

 This verse calls for patience and gentleness in relationships, emphasising the importance of enduring challenges with love and understanding.

Interpretation

 In marriage, patience is crucial during difficult seasons, disagreements, or times of waiting. Choosing patience allows couples to navigate struggles with grace, avoiding frustration or anger. It's an expression of love that mirrors God's long-suffering patience with us.

CORRELATION

 1 Corinthians 13:4 reminds us, "Love is patient, love is kind." True love demonstrates patience, especially in moments of weakness or trial.

REFLECTION

- Are you patient with each other during stressful times?
- How can you remind yourselves to respond with grace instead of frustration?

CHALLENGE

 This week, commit to responding with patience in moments of stress or disagreement. Take a deep breath, say a silent prayer, and remind yourself to choose gentleness and understanding.

PRAYER

Father, thank You for Your patience with us. Teach us to show that same patience in our marriage, especially during challenging moments. Help us bear with each other in love, growing closer every season. In Jesus' name, Amen.

WEEK 19

19

Celebrating Your Differences

"For just as each of us has one body with many members, and these members do not all have the same function, so in Christ we, though many, form one body."

ROMANS 12:4-5 (NIV)

OBSERVATION

 This passage acknowledges that diversity is part of God's design. Each person is unique, and these differences contribute to the greater good when embraced with love and respect.

INTERPRETATION

 In marriage, spouses bring different personalities, strengths, and perspectives. Instead of letting differences cause division, couples can celebrate them as complementary gifts. Understanding and appreciating each other's uniqueness fosters unity and harmony.

CORRELATION

1 Corinthians 12:12-14 compares the body of Christ to a single body with many parts, emphasising how differences work together for a greater purpose. This principle applies beautifully to marriage.

REFLECTION

* Do you view your differences as strengths or challenges?
* How can you use your unique traits to strengthen your partnership?

CHALLENGE

This week, identify one quality in your spouse that's different from your own and express appreciation for how it benefits your relationship. Celebrate the ways your differences make you a stronger team.

PRAYER

Lord, thank You for creating us with unique gifts and perspectives. Please help us to appreciate and celebrate our differences as a couple, using them to build a stronger and more unified marriage. In Jesus' name, Amen.

WEEK 20

20

Pursuing Spiritual Growth Together

*"But grow in the grace and knowledge
of our Lord and Savior Jesus Christ.
To him be glory both now and forever!"*

2 PETER 3:18 (NIV)

OBSERVATION

 This verse emphasises the importance of continual spiritual growth, both individually and as a couple. Pursuing God's grace and knowledge strengthens faith and brings glory to Him.

INTERPRETATION

 Couples who grow spiritually together deepen their connection with each other and with God. Building habits such as prayer, Bible study, and worship strengthens the foundation of marriage and helps couples face life's challenges with faith and wisdom.

CORRELATION

 Psalm 1:2-3 describes the one who delights in God's Word as being like a tree planted by streams of water, yielding fruit in season. A marriage rooted in God's Word is similarly fruitful and enduring.

REFLECTION

* How can you prioritise spiritual growth as a couple?
* Are you consistently making time for God in your relationship?

CHALLENGE

 Set aside time this week to study the Bible or pray together. Choose a passage or devotional to read, and share what God is teaching you. Commit to making this a regular habit in your marriage.

PRAYER

Father, thank You for the opportunity to grow in grace and knowledge together. Help us to seek You daily and make You the foundation of our marriage. May our spiritual growth strengthen our relationship and glorify You. In Jesus' name, Amen.

WEEK 21

The Beauty of Encouragement

*"Therefore encourage one another
and build each other up,
just as in fact you are doing."*

1 THESSALONIANS 5:11 (NIV)

OBSERVATION

 This verse highlights the importance of encouragement in relationships. Building each other up fosters confidence, hope, and perseverance.

INTERPRETATION

 Marriage thrives on mutual encouragement. Kind words, affirmations, and support strengthen emotional and spiritual bonds. When couples actively encourage one another, they create an environment where love and growth flourish.

CORRELATION

 Hebrews 10:24 says, "And let us consider how we may spur one another on toward love and good deeds." Encouragement is an essential part of fulfilling God's design for relationships.

REFLECTION

* Are you intentional about encouraging each other in your daily lives?
* How can you make encouragement a regular practice in your marriage?

CHALLENGE

 Each day this week, find one way to encourage your spouse—whether through a compliment, a note of appreciation, or words of affirmation. Observe how these small acts of encouragement impact your relationship.

PRAYER

Lord, thank You for the power of encouragement. Help us to build each other up and speak words of love and affirmation. May our encouragement reflect Your love and inspire us to grow closer to You and each other. In Jesus' name, Amen.

WEEK 22

Trusting God in Uncertainty

*"Trust in the Lord with all your heart
and lean not on your own understanding;
in all your ways submit to him,
and he will make your paths straight."*

PROVERBS 3:5-6 (NIV)

OBSERVATION

 This verse reminds us to place our trust in God, especially when facing uncertainties. Trusting Him means letting go of the need for control and relying on His wisdom and guidance.

INTERPRETATION

 In marriage, seasons of uncertainty—financial challenges, health issues, or major decisions—can create stress. Trusting God together helps couples navigate these times with peace and unity. By submitting to God's will, you invite Him to guide your path and strengthen your relationship.

CORRELATION

Isaiah 26:3 says, "You will keep in perfect peace those whose minds are steadfast because they trust in you." Trusting God brings peace and stability, even in turbulent times.

REFLECTION

* Are there areas in your marriage where you need to trust God more?
* How can you encourage each other to rely on His promises during uncertain times?

CHALLENGE

This week, identify one area of uncertainty in your life. Commit to praying about it together daily, asking God for wisdom and peace. Trust Him to guide your steps as a couple.

PRAYER

Lord, thank You for being our refuge and guide in uncertain times. Help us to trust You completely and lean on Your wisdom instead of our own understanding. May we seek Your will in every decision and grow closer to You through it. In Jesus' name, Amen.

WEEK 23

23

Honoring Each Other's Needs

"Do nothing out of selfish ambition or vain conceit. Rather, in humility value others above yourselves, not looking to your own interests but each of you to the interests of the others."
PHILIPPIANS 2:3-4 (NIV)

OBSERVATION

 This passage calls for humility and selflessness in relationships. It encourages us to prioritise others' needs and to honour them with love and care.

INTERPRETATION

 In marriage, honouring your spouse's needs means setting aside selfish desires to serve and love them intentionally. When both partners live out this principle, it creates an environment of mutual respect, trust, and deeper connection.

CORRELATION

 Galatians 5:13 says, "Serve one another humbly in love." Marriage thrives when spouses choose to serve and prioritise each other selflessly.

REFLECTION

* Are you attentive to each other's needs, both big and small?
* How can you better serve one another in love this week?

CHALLENGE

 Ask your spouse, "What can I do to serve you this week?" Commit to fulfilling their request joyfully. Reflect on how this simple act of service strengthens your bond.

PRAYER

Father, thank You for the example of humility and service in Jesus. Help us to value each other's needs above our own and to serve one another with love and joy. May our marriage reflect Your selfless love. In Jesus' name, Amen.

WEEK 24

Building a Foundation of Faith

*"Unless the Lord builds the house,
the builders labor in vain."*

Psalm 127:1 (NIV)

OBSERVATION

 This verse reminds us that our efforts are fruitless without God at the center of our lives and relationships. A strong foundation is built on faith and dependence on Him.

INTERPRETATION

 In marriage, God must be the cornerstone of your relationship. When couples prioritise their faith and allow God to guide their decisions, their marriage becomes a reflection of His love and glory. Building a foundation of faith equips you to withstand life's challenges together.

CORRELATION

Matthew 7:24-25 speaks of the wise man who built his house on the rock, a solid foundation that withstood storms. A marriage rooted in Christ provides the same stability.

REFLECTION

* Is God at the centre of your marriage?
* How can you strengthen your spiritual foundation as a couple?

CHALLENGE

This week, reflect on ways you can keep God as the foundation of your marriage. Begin or renew a habit of praying together daily and committing your plans to Him.

PRAYER

Lord, thank You for being the foundation of our marriage. Help us to build our lives on Your Word and Your truth. Strengthen our faith and guide us in every decision. May our marriage bring You glory. In Jesus' name, Amen.

WEEK 25

25

Choosing Love Over Anger

"My dear brothers and sisters, take note of this: Everyone should be quick to listen, slow to speak, and slow to become angry, because human anger does not produce the righteousness that God desires."

JAMES 1:19-20 (NIV)

OBSERVATION

 This verse teaches the value of listening and exercising self-control. It warns against the destructive effects of unchecked anger and emphasises the importance of responding with love and understanding.

INTERPRETATION

 In marriage, anger can damage trust and communication if not appropriately managed. Choosing love over anger requires patience, active listening, and a commitment to gracefully resolving conflict. This brings peace and nurtures a healthy relationship.

CORRELATION

Proverbs 15:1 says, "A gentle answer turns away wrath, but a harsh word stirs up anger." Gentleness and patience defuse tension, promoting reconciliation instead of division.

REFLECTION

* How do you handle anger in your relationship?
* Are you quick to listen and slow to speak when conflicts arise?

CHALLENGE

This week, focus on responding with gentleness during disagreements. Practice active listening by paraphrasing your spouse's concerns before replying. Reflect on how this approach improves communication.

PRAYER

Lord, thank You for teaching us to respond with love instead of anger. Please help us to be patient, gentle, and understanding in our words and actions. May Your peace reign in our marriage. In Jesus' name, Amen.

WEEK 26

A Love That Perseveres

"Love always protects, always trusts, always hopes, always perseveres."

1 CORINTHIANS 13:7 (NIV)

OBSERVATION

 This verse describes the enduring and selfless nature of true love. Love is not passive; it actively protects, trusts, hopes, and perseveres through all circumstances.

INTERPRETATION

 Marriage is a journey that requires perseverance. True love doesn't give up when challenges arise; it holds on, trusting in God's faithfulness and the strength of your commitment. By protecting and nurturing your relationship, you reflect God's enduring love.

CORRELATION

Romans 12:12 says, "Be joyful in hope, patient in affliction, faithful in prayer." Perseverance in marriage is strengthened by hope, patience, and prayer.

REFLECTION

* How can you persevere through challenges together with love and faith?
* Are you trusting God to sustain you during difficult seasons?

CHALLENGE

Reflect on a past challenge you overcame together. Thank God for His faithfulness, and discuss how you can approach future trials with the same perseverance and trust in Him.

PRAYER

Father, thank You for Your unwavering love that perseveres through all things. Help us to reflect that love in our marriage by protecting, trusting, hoping, and persevering together. Strengthen us in every season. In Jesus' name, Amen.

WEEK 27

The Power of Gratitude

*"Give thanks in all circumstances;
for this is God's will for you in Christ Jesus."*

1 THESSALONIANS 5:18 (NIV)

OBSERVATION

 This verse calls believers to maintain a heart of gratitude in every situation, trusting that God's plan is good and His presence is constant.

INTERPRETATION

 Gratitude transforms relationships. In marriage, choosing to focus on blessings instead of challenges fosters joy and strengthens your bond. A grateful heart recognises your spouse's gift and God's grace at work in your lives.

CORRELATION

 Philippians 4:6 says, "Do not be anxious about anything, but in every situation, by prayer and petition, with thanksgiving, present your requests to God." Gratitude is a vital part of finding peace and contentment in all circumstances.

REFLECTION

* Do you regularly express gratitude for each other and God's blessings?
* How can a habit of gratitude shape your perspective in tough times?

CHALLENGE

 Take turns this week sharing three things you are grateful for each day. Include at least one thing about your spouse. Let this practice build a deeper appreciation for each other and God's provision.

PRAYER

Lord, thank You for the many blessings You have poured into our lives. Teach us to be grateful in all circumstances and to see Your hand at work in our marriage. May our gratitude glorify You and strengthen our bond. In Jesus' name, Amen.

WEEK 28

Speaking Life Into Your Marriage

"The tongue has the power of life and death, and those who love it will eat its fruit."

PROVERBS 18:21 (NIV)

Observation

 This verse underscores the incredible power of words. What we say can build others up or tear them down, shaping the relationships around us.

Interpretation

 In marriage, words carry weight. Speaking life into your spouse means offering encouragement, love, and affirmation rather than criticism or negativity. When couples are intentional with their words, their marriage becomes a source of joy and healing.

CORRELATION

Ephesians 4:29 says, "Do not let any unwholesome talk come out of your mouths, but only what is helpful for building others up according to their needs." Words should always aim to uplift and strengthen.

REFLECTION

* Are your words building each other up or tearing each other down?
* How can you speak more life-giving words in your daily conversations?

CHALLENGE

This week, focus on giving your spouse genuine compliments and affirmations daily. Avoid speaking words of frustration or criticism, even in difficult moments. Reflect on how this intentional shift impacts your relationship.

PRAYER

Father, thank You for the power of words and the ability to speak life into our marriage. Please help us to use our words to encourage and uplift one another. May our conversations reflect Your love and bring healing and joy. In Jesus' name, Amen.

WEEK 29

Walking in Humility

*"Clothe yourselves, all of you,
with humility toward one another,
for 'God opposes the proud but
gives grace to the humble.'"*

1 PETER 5:5 (ESV)

OBSERVATION

 This verse highlights the importance of humility in relationships, reminding us that God blesses those with humble hearts.

INTERPRETATION

 In marriage, humility means setting aside pride to prioritise your spouse's needs and being willing to admit when you're wrong. Humility fosters peace and understanding, creating an environment where love can thrive.

CORRELATION

 Philippians 2:5 reminds us, "In your relationships with one another, have the same mindset as Christ Jesus." Christ's humility serves as the ultimate model for how we should treat one another.

REFLECTION

* Are there areas in your marriage where pride hinders your connection?
* How can you grow in humility to better serve and love each other?

CHALLENGE

 This week, identify one area where pride may have caused tension in your relationship. Humbly apologise or seek forgiveness, and take one step toward restoring peace.

PRAYER

 Lord, thank You for showing us perfect humility through Jesus. Teach us to set aside pride and walk humbly with each other. Help us to serve one another in love and reflect Your grace in our marriage. In Jesus' name, Amen.

WEEK 30

Resting in God's Peace

*"Peace I leave with you; my peace I give you.
I do not give to you as the world gives.
Do not let your hearts be troubled
and do not be afraid."*

JOHN 14:27 (NIV)

OBSERVATION

 Jesus offers a peace that surpasses worldly understanding. It is a peace rooted in His presence and promises, providing rest for troubled hearts.

INTERPRETATION

 In marriage, it's easy to become overwhelmed by life's demands or conflicts. Seeking God's peace together creates a haven where you can find rest and reassurance in your relationship. His peace strengthens your unity and calms the storms you face.

CORRELATION

Philippians 4:7 says, "And the peace of God, which transcends all understanding, will guard your hearts and your minds in Christ Jesus." God's peace is a powerful guard against fear and anxiety in your marriage.

REFLECTION

* Are you seeking God's peace together during stressful times?
* How can you create an atmosphere of peace in your home?

CHALLENGE

This week, set aside time to rest in God's presence together. Whether through prayer, worship or simply a quiet moment, invite His peace into your marriage and your home.

PRAYER

Father, thank You for the peace that only You can give. Help us to rest in Your promises and trust You with our worries. May Your peace fill our hearts and home, drawing us closer to You and each other. In Jesus' name, Amen.

WEEK 31

Serving Each Other in Love

"You, my brothers and sisters, were called to be free. But do not use your freedom to indulge the flesh; rather, serve one another humbly in love."

GALATIANS 5:13 (NIV)

OBSERVATION

 This verse emphasises the Christian call to serve one another selflessly. True love is shown through humble acts of service, reflecting the love of Christ.

INTERPRETATION

 In marriage, serving your spouse is a tangible expression of love. It's not about keeping score or meeting obligations but about joyfully putting their needs ahead of yours. This selfless mindset fosters deeper intimacy and reflects God's love in your relationship.

CORRELATION

John 13:14-15 illustrates this principle as Jesus washed His disciples' feet, teaching them the humility and joy of serving one another.

REFLECTION

* Do you serve each other with joyful hearts or serve reluctantly?
* How can you better prioritise your spouse's needs this week?

CHALLENGE

Perform one intentional act of service for your spouse each day this week. Whether it's taking on a chore, offering a small gesture of kindness, or meeting an unspoken need, let these acts communicate your love.

PRAYER

Lord, thank You for the example of the humble service You gave us. Teach us to serve one another with love and joy. May our service draw us closer to each other and glorify You in our marriage. In Jesus' name, Amen.

WEEK 32

32

Building Trust Through Faithfulness

"Let love and faithfulness never leave you; bind them around your neck, write them on the tablet of your heart. Then you will win favor and a good name in the sight of God and man."

PROVERBS 3:3-4 (NIV)

OBSERVATION

 This passage highlights the enduring qualities of love and faithfulness. These virtues not only strengthen relationships but also honour God.

INTERPRETATION

 Trust is the foundation of a strong marriage, and it's built through consistent faithfulness in words, actions, and intentions. When couples commit to love and faithfulness, they create a bond that reflects the steadfast love of God.

CORRELATION

Lamentations 3:22-23 says, "Because of the Lord's great love we are not consumed, for his compassions never fail. They are new every morning; great is Your faithfulness." God's unwavering faithfulness serves as a model for how we should treat one another.

REFLECTION

* Are you consistently showing love and faithfulness in your actions and words?
* How can you rebuild or strengthen trust in areas where it may have faltered?

CHALLENGE

Evaluate your daily actions and words to ensure they align with love and faithfulness. If there's an area where trust has been strained, take steps to rebuild it this week through honest communication and consistent actions.

PRAYER

Father, thank You for Your steadfast love and faithfulness. Help us to reflect these qualities in our marriage, building trust and honouring You. Strengthen our commitment to each other and deepen our love. In Jesus' name, Amen.

WEEK 33

33

Practicing Contentment

"Keep your lives free from the love of money and be content with what you have, because God has said, Never will I leave you; never will I forsake you.'"

HEBREWS 13:5 (NIV)

OBSERVATION

 This verse encourages believers to cultivate contentment, trusting God's provision and presence rather than material wealth.

INTERPRETATION

 Discontentment can strain a marriage, especially when it comes to financial or material concerns. Practising contentment allows couples to focus on the blessings they already have and trust God to provide for their needs. This fosters peace and gratitude in the relationship.

CORRELATION

Philippians 4:11-12 teaches us to be content in all circumstances, relying on Christ for strength. This mindset transforms how couples approach challenges and blessings alike.

REFLECTION

* Are you focusing on what you have or what you lack?
* How can you cultivate a spirit of gratitude and contentment in our marriage?

CHALLENGE

This week, discuss the blessings you are thankful for as a couple. Avoid comparing your situation to others, and focus on ways to simplify and embrace contentment together.

PRAYER

Lord, thank You for Your faithful provision in our lives. Teach us to be content with what You have given us and to trust You with our needs. May we find joy in gratitude and simplicity. In Jesus' name, Amen.

WEEK 34

34

Rejoicing in Hope

*"Be joyful in hope,
patient in affliction,
faithful in prayer."*

ROMANS 12:12 (NIV)

OBSERVATION

 This verse calls believers to embrace joy, patience, and prayer as essential practices, especially in times of difficulty.

INTERPRETATION

 Hope is a powerful force in marriage. It sustains couples during trials, reminding them that God's promises are true and His plans are good. Rejoicing in hope strengthens your bond as you face challenges together with faith and optimism.

CORRELATION

Psalm 33:18-19 reminds us, "The eyes of the Lord are on those who fear Him, on those whose hope is in His unfailing love." Hope anchored in God's love provides stability and joy in every season.

REFLECTION

* Are you placing your hope in God's promises or discouraged by circumstances?
* How can you practice joy and patience during trials?

CHALLENGE

This week, focus on encouraging one another with reminders of God's faithfulness. Share a or personal story of hope each day to uplift and inspire each other.

PRAYER

Father, thank You for the hope we have in You. Help us to rejoice in Your promises and to face every challenge with patience and faith. May Your hope fill our hearts and strengthen our marriage. In Jesus' name, Amen.

WEEK 35

Fostering Unity Through Peace

"Make every effort to keep the unity of the Spirit through the bond of peace."

EPHESIANS 4:3 (NIV)

OBSERVATION

 This verse emphasises the importance of maintaining unity, which is nurtured by peace and guided by the Spirit of God.

INTERPRETATION

 Unity in marriage requires effort, especially when conflicts arise. Seeking peace doesn't mean avoiding problems but addressing them with humility and love. When couples strive for unity, their marriage reflects God's harmony and grace.

CORRELATION

 Colossians 3:14-15 says, "And over all these virtues put on love, which binds them all together in perfect unity. Let the peace of Christ rule in your hearts." Love and peace are the foundation of unity in relationships.

REFLECTION

* Are you striving for unity or letting conflicts divide you?
* How can you foster a spirit of peace in your home and relationship?

CHALLENGE

 This week, address any unresolved conflicts with the goal of reconciliation and peace. Commit to listening without interrupting, apologising when needed, and prioritising unity over being "right."

PRAYER

Lord, thank You for the gift of unity through Your Spirit. Help us to seek peace in our marriage and to resolve conflicts with humility and love. May our bond reflect Your grace and harmony. In Jesus' name, Amen.

WEEK 36

Forgiving as Christ Forgave

"Bear with each other and forgive one another if any of you has a grievance against someone. Forgive as the Lord forgave you."

COLOSSIANS 3:13 (NIV)

OBSERVATION

 This verse reminds believers of the central role forgiveness plays in relationships. Just as Christ forgives us unconditionally, we are called to extend that same forgiveness to others.

INTERPRETATION

 In marriage, forgiveness is essential for healing and growth. Holding onto resentment creates division, but choosing to forgive reflects God's love and grace. When couples forgive each other as Christ forgives, they cultivate a relationship rooted in mercy and understanding.

Correlation

Ephesians 4:32 reinforces this principle: "Be kind and compassionate to one another, forgiving each other, just as in Christ God forgave you." Forgiveness is a key expression of love and compassion in marriage.

Reflection

* Are there past hurts you need to forgive each other for?
* How can you extend grace to one another, even when it's difficult?

Challenge

This week, reflect on any unresolved grievances or frustrations in your marriage. Openly discuss these with your spouse, offering and asking for forgiveness where needed. Trust God to bring healing and restoration.

Prayer

Lord, thank You for Your unfailing forgiveness toward us. Teach us to forgive one another as You forgive, letting go of bitterness and embracing grace. Heal any wounds in our marriage and help us to reflect Your mercy. In Jesus' name, Amen.

WEEK 37

Loving Through Sacrifice

*"Greater love has no one than this:
to lay down one's life for one's friends."*
JOHN 15:13 (NIV)

OBSERVATION

This verse describes the depth of sacrificial love, modelled perfectly by Jesus. True love involves selflessness and a willingness to put others' needs above yours.

INTERPRETATION

Marriage calls for sacrificial love—a love that puts your spouse's well-being ahead of your preferences. Sacrifice might mean giving up time, energy, or comfort to support and care for each other. This kind of love strengthens your bond and mirrors the love of Christ.

CORRELATION

 Ephesians 5:25 illustrates this in the context of marriage: "Husbands, love your wives, just as Christ loved the church and gave himself up for her." This sacrificial love is the cornerstone of a Christ-centered marriage.

REFLECTION

* Are you willing to make sacrifices for each other's benefit?
* How can you show sacrificial love in the daily routines of your marriage?

CHALLENGE

 Identify one way you can sacrifice for your spouse this week, whether it's your time, comfort, or preferences. Let this act demonstrate your love and commitment to their happiness and well-being.

PRAYER

Father, thank You for the ultimate example of sacrificial love in Jesus. Help us love each other selflessly, putting our needs above our own. May our love reflect the depth of Your love. In Jesus' name, Amen.

WEEK 38

Renewing Your Mind Together

"Do not conform to the pattern of this world, but be transformed by the renewing of your mind. Then you will be able to test and approve what God's will is—His good, pleasing and perfect will."

ROMANS 12:2 (NIV)

OBSERVATION

 This verse encourages believers to reject worldly influences and instead seek transformation through the renewing of their minds in God's Word and will.

INTERPRETATION

 In marriage, renewing your mind together strengthens your spiritual connection and alignment with God's purpose. Regularly studying Scripture and praying as a couple keeps your thoughts and actions centred on Christ.

CORRELATION

 Philippians 4:8 guides believers to focus on what is true, noble, right, pure, lovely, and admirable—qualities that shape a Christ-centered mindset in marriage.

REFLECTION

* Are you prioritising time to grow spiritually together?
* How can you encourage each other to renew their minds through Scripture and prayer?

CHALLENGE

 Commit to a shared devotional or Bible study this week. Dedicate time to discuss how God is speaking to you both and pray for His guidance in your marriage.

PRAYER

Lord, thank You for the gift of transformation through Your Word. Help us to renew our minds together, focusing on Your truth and aligning our lives with Your will. Strengthen our bond as we grow closer to You. In Jesus' name, Amen.

WEEK 39

Strength in Weakness

"But He said to me, 'My grace is sufficient for you, for my power is made perfect in weakness.' Therefore, I will boast all the more gladly about my weaknesses, so that Christ's power may rest on me."

2 CORINTHIANS 12:9 (NIV)

OBSERVATION

 This verse reminds us that God's grace is sufficient in all circumstances, and His power is magnified in our weakness.

INTERPRETATION

 In marriage, admitting weaknesses can be challenging, but it opens the door for God's grace to work in and through your relationship. Leaning on His strength allows you to overcome challenges together and grow closer in dependence on Him.

CORRELATION

 Isaiah 40:29 says, "He gives strength to the weary and increases the power of the weak." God's strength is always available to sustain and uplift couples in their times of need.

REFLECTION

* Are you relying on God's grace in your weaknesses, or are you trying to handle everything on your own?
* How can you support each other in times of struggle?

CHALLENGE

 This week, share a personal struggle or weakness with your spouse. Pray together for God's strength and grace to work in that area. Encourage each other to trust Him fully.

PRAYER

Lord, thank You for Your grace, which is sufficient in every weakness. Help us to rely on Your strength and support each other in times of struggle. May Your power work in and through our marriage. In Jesus' name, Amen.

WEEK 40

Bearing Fruit Together

*"I am the vine; you are the branches.
If you remain in me and I in you, you will bear
much fruit; apart from me you can do nothing."*
JOHN 15:5 (NIV)

OBSERVATION

 This verse emphasises the importance of staying connected to Christ to bear spiritual fruit. Apart from Him, our efforts are unproductive.

INTERPRETATION

 In marriage, staying connected to Christ allows you to bear fruit together—love, joy, peace, patience, and other fruits of the Spirit. A Christ-centered marriage becomes a witness of His goodness to others.

CORRELATION

Galatians 5:22-23 outlines the fruit of the Spirit: "Love, joy, peace, forbearance, kindness, goodness, faithfulness, gentleness, and self-control." These qualities strengthen and sustain a godly marriage.

REFLECTION

* Are you staying rooted in Christ individually and as a couple?

* How can you cultivate more spiritual fruit in your relationship?

CHALLENGE

This week, focus on one fruit of the Spirit you want to grow in as a couple. Practice it intentionally in your interactions, and pray for God to strengthen your relationship.

PRAYER

Lord, thank You for being the vine that sustains us. Help us remain in You, bearing fruit that glorifies and strengthens our marriage. May our love and unity reflect Your Spirit. In Jesus' name, Amen.

WEEK 41

Facing Trials Together

"Consider it pure joy, my brothers and sisters, whenever you face trials of many kinds, because you know that the testing of your faith produces perseverance."

JAMES 1:2-3 (NIV)

OBSERVATION

 This verse highlights the purpose of trials, showing that challenges refine faith and build perseverance, leading to spiritual growth.

INTERPRETATION

 Marriage is not free from trials, but facing challenges together can strengthen your bond and deepen your faith. When you see trials as opportunities to grow as individuals and as a couple, you can navigate difficulties with hope and trust in God.

CORRELATION

Romans 5:3-5 reinforces this: "Not only so, but we also glory in our sufferings, because we know that suffering produces perseverance; perseverance, character; and character, hope." Trials are part of God's refining work in your lives.

REFLECTION

* How do you usually respond to trials in your marriage?
* How can you better trust God and grow stronger together during difficult seasons?

CHALLENGE

Identify a current or past trial you've faced as a couple. Reflect on how God has worked through it or is working now. Pray together, thanking Him for His guidance and asking for strength to persevere.

PRAYER

Lord, thank You for using trials to refine and strengthen us. Help us to face challenges with joy, trusting in Your plan and relying on Your strength. May our faith and perseverance grow, bringing us closer to each other and to You. In Jesus' name, Amen.

WEEK 42

Embracing Your Roles

"Submit to one another out of reverence for Christ."

EPHESIANS 5:21 (NIV)

OBSERVATION

 This verse emphasises mutual submission in marriage, guided by love and respect for Christ. It reminds couples that marriage is a partnership rooted in service and humility.

INTERPRETATION

 God designed marriage as a reflection of His love, with each spouse embracing their unique role. Submission is not about control but about serving each other selflessly. When both partners respect and support one another, their relationship honours God.

CORRELATION

 1 Peter 3:7 adds, "Husbands, in the same way, be considerate as you live with your wives, and treat them with respect as the weaker partner and as heirs with you of the gracious gift of life." This mutual respect strengthens unity.

REFLECTION

* Are you serving and supporting each other in your God-given roles?
* How can you better reflect Christ's humility and love in your partnership?

CHALLENGE

 Discuss your individual roles in your marriage this week. Identify one area where you can better support or serve your spouse, and commit to doing so.

PRAYER

Father, thank You for the gift of marriage and the unique roles You have given us. Help us to serve and support one another in love, reflecting Christ's humility and grace. May our partnership glorify You. In Jesus' name, Amen.

WEEK 43

Practicing Kindness Daily

"Be kind and compassionate to one another, forgiving each other, just as in Christ God forgave you."

EPHESIANS 4:32 (NIV)

OBSERVATION

 This verse highlights the importance of kindness and compassion in relationships, rooted in the example of Christ's forgiveness and love.

INTERPRETATION

 Kindness is a simple yet powerful way to show love in marriage. Small acts of compassion and thoughtfulness build a strong foundation of trust and affection. When kindness is practised daily, it fosters a loving and nurturing environment.

CORRELATION

 Proverbs 16:24 says, "Gracious words are a honeycomb, sweet to the soul and healing to the bones." Words and actions filled with kindness bring healing and joy to your relationship.

REFLECTION

* Are you consistently showing kindness to one another, even in small ways?
* How can you be more intentional about practising compassion in our daily lives?

CHALLENGE

 This week, focus on one act of kindness for your spouse each day. It could be a thoughtful note, a small gift, or a simple gesture like making their favourite meal. Observe how these acts impact your connection.

PRAYER

Lord, thank You for Your endless kindness and compassion toward us. Teach us to reflect that kindness in our marriage, creating an atmosphere of love and grace. Please help us to prioritise kindness daily. In Jesus' name, Amen.

WEEK 44

Guarding Your Hearts

*"Above all else, guard your heart,
for everything you do flows from it."*
PROVERBS 4:23 (NIV)

OBSERVATION

 This verse emphasises the importance of protecting your heart from negative influences as they shape your thoughts, actions, and relationships.

INTERPRETATION

 In marriage, guarding your heart means being intentional about what you allow to influence your relationship. Protecting your heart ensures that your marriage remains centered on love and faithfulness, whether it's unhealthy habits, harmful words, or distractions.

CORRELATION

Philippians 4:7 reminds us that "the peace of God, which transcends all understanding, will guard your hearts and your minds in Christ Jesus." Relying on God's peace helps shield your relationship from negativity.

REFLECTION

* Are there influences or habits that may be negatively affecting your marriage?
* How can you guard your hearts and prioritise God's truth in your relationship?

CHALLENGE

Identify one distraction or negative influence you can eliminate this week to protect your marriage better. Replace it with a positive habit or practice that strengthens your bond.

PRAYER

Lord, thank You for the gift of our hearts and the love we share. Help us guard our hearts and minds, freeing our marriage from harmful influences. May Your peace guide us and protect our relationship. In Jesus' name, Amen.

WEEK 45

Being Patient in Love

*"Love is patient, love is kind.
It does not envy,
it does not boast, it is not proud."*

1 CORINTHIANS 13:4 (NIV)

OBSERVATION

 This verse defines love through patience and kindness, qualities that sustain healthy and enduring relationships.

INTERPRETATION

 Patience is a cornerstone of love in marriage. It requires understanding, grace, and a willingness to endure challenges without frustration. Practising patience shows your spouse that you value them and prioritise the health of your relationship over temporary irritations.

CORRELATION

 Proverbs 15:18 says, "A hot-tempered person stirs up conflict, but the one who is patient calms a quarrel." Patience leads to peace and resolution in times of conflict.

REFLECTION

* Are you showing patience to each other, especially in difficult moments?

* How can we grow in this aspect of love in our marriage?

CHALLENGE

 This week, practice patience during moments of frustration. Pause before reacting, take a deep breath and respond with understanding and kindness. Reflect on how this changes the dynamic in your relationship.

PRAYER

Father, thank You for Your patience with us. Teach us to extend that same patience to one another, even in challenging moments. Help us to love with grace and understanding. In Jesus' name, Amen.

WEEK 46

46

Speaking Life into Your Marriage

"The tongue has the power of life and death, and those who love it will eat its fruit."

PROVERBS 18:21 (NIV)

OBSERVATION

 This verse emphasises the immense power of words, which can either build up or tear down relationships. Words have lasting impacts and reveal the condition of the heart.

INTERPRETATION

 In marriage, the way you speak to each other matters. Words of encouragement, love, and affirmation bring life and strength to your relationship. Harsh or careless words, however, can create wounds. Speaking life into your marriage requires mindfulness and a commitment to uplifting communication.

CORRELATION

Colossians 4:6 encourages believers: "Let your conversation be always full of grace, seasoned with salt, so that you may know how to answer everyone." Grace-filled words nurture healthy relationships.

REFLECTION

* Are your words building each other up or tearing each other down?

* How can you create an atmosphere of encouragement and love through your conversations?

CHALLENGE

This week, intentionally speak words of affirmation and encouragement to your spouse daily. Avoid negative or critical comments, even in frustration, and focus on uplifting each other.

PRAYER

Lord, thank You for the gift of communication. Please help us to use our words to build each other up and strengthen our marriage. Let our conversations be full of grace, reflecting Your love. In Jesus' name, Amen.

WEEK 47

Rejoicing in Your Spouse

*"Let your fountain be blessed,
and rejoice in the wife of your youth."*
PROVERBS 5:18 (ESV)

OBSERVATION

 This verse encourages delighting in the blessing of marriage and finding joy in your spouse. It celebrates love, companionship, and the deep connection God designed for marriage.

INTERPRETATION

 Rejoicing in your spouse means appreciating and celebrating them daily. It's about cherishing their unique qualities and the bond you share. This attitude fosters gratitude and intimacy, drawing you closer together.

CORRELATION

 Ecclesiastes 9:9 also advises, "Enjoy life with your wife, whom you love, all the days of this meaningless life that God has given you under the sun." Joy in marriage is a gift from God that is to be treasured.

REFLECTION

* Are you taking time to celebrate and appreciate each other?
* How can you cultivate more joy and gratitude in your relationship?

CHALLENGE

 Plan a special date or activity this week to celebrate your spouse. Share specific things you appreciate about them and express your gratitude for their presence in your life.

PRAYER

Lord, thank You for the gift of my spouse and the joy we share. Help us to rejoice in one another, appreciating the blessing of our marriage. May our love reflect Your goodness and grace. In Jesus' name, Amen.

WEEK 48

48

Trusting God's Plan for Your Marriage

"For I know the plans I have for you," declares the Lord, "plans to prosper you and not to harm you, plans to give you hope and a future."

JEREMIAH 29:11 (NIV)

OBSERVATION

 This verse reminds us that God's plans are good and filled with hope. Trusting Him brings peace, even when the future is uncertain.

INTERPRETATION

 In marriage, there are seasons of uncertainty and challenge, but trusting in God's plan ensures you face them with hope. Together, you can lean on His promises, knowing He is working all things for your good.

CORRELATION

 Proverbs 3:5-6 advises, "Trust in the Lord with all your heart and lean not on your own understanding; in all your ways submit to Him, and He will make your paths straight." Trusting God aligns your marriage with His perfect will.

REFLECTION

- Are you trusting God's plan for your marriage, even in difficult times?
- How can you grow in faith and rely on His promises together?

CHALLENGE

 Spend time praying together this week about your future as a couple. Surrender your plans to God and ask for His guidance and blessing in the days ahead.

PRAYER

 Lord, thank You for your plans for our lives and marriage. Help us trust You fully, knowing Your ways are good and hopeful. Guide us as we walk together in faith. In Jesus' name, Amen.

WEEK 49

Celebrating Unity

*"Though one may be overpowered,
two can defend themselves.
A cord of three strands
is not quickly broken."*

ECCLESIASTES 4:12 (NIV)

OBSERVATION

 This verse illustrates the strength found in unity, especially when God is at the centre of a relationship.

INTERPRETATION

 A marriage anchored in unity is powerful and enduring. When both spouses are united, and God is their foundation, they can withstand challenges and grow stronger together. Unity requires mutual commitment, communication, and faith.

CORRELATION

Psalm 133:1 declares, "How good and pleasant it is when God's people live together in unity!" Unity is a blessing that reflects God's design for relationships.

REFLECTION

* Are you striving for unity in our marriage, or are there areas where division needs to be addressed?

* How can we invite God to strengthen the unity in our relationship?

CHALLENGE

This week, work together to resolve any areas of disagreement or division. Pray for God's guidance and focus on building unity in your relationship.

PRAYER

Lord, thank You for the gift of unity in marriage. Help us to grow closer to each other and to You, creating a bond that cannot be broken. Strengthen our love and commitment, reflecting Your perfect unity. In Jesus' name, Amen.

WEEK 50

50

Serving Together

*"As each has received a gift,
use it to serve one another,
as good stewards of God's varied grace."*

1 PETER 4:10 (ESV)

OBSERVATION

 This verse emphasises the importance of using God-given gifts to serve others, fostering love and gratitude.

INTERPRETATION

 In marriage, serving together allows you to share your gifts with the world while strengthening your bond. Whether through ministry, acts of kindness, or helping your community, serving reflects God's love and purpose for your relationship.

CORRELATION

 Matthew 20:28 reminds us of Jesus' example: "The Son of Man did not come to be served, but to serve." Serving together mirrors His humility and love.

REFLECTION

* Are you using your gifts to serve each other and those around us?
* How can serving together deepen your connection and glorify God?

CHALLENGE

 Choose a service activity to do together this week—volunteer at church, help a neighbour or support a charitable cause. Reflect on how this strengthens your relationship and faith.

PRAYER

Lord, thank You for the gifts You've given us. Please help us to use them to serve each other and those around us. May our marriage reflect Your grace and love as we serve together. In Jesus' name, Amen.

WEEK 51

Forgiveness in Action

"Bear with each other and forgive one another if any of you has a grievance against someone. Forgive as the Lord forgave you."

COLOSSIANS 3:13 (NIV)

OBSERVATION

 This verse calls us to extend forgiveness, just as Christ has forgiven us. Forgiveness is a cornerstone of grace-filled relationships.

INTERPRETATION

 In marriage, forgiveness is essential to healing and growth. Holding onto grievances creates distance while choosing forgiveness fosters love and unity. Reflecting Christ's forgiveness enables couples to overcome hurt and grow stronger together.

CORRELATION

 Matthew 6:14-15 reminds us, "For if you forgive other people when they sin against you, your heavenly Father will also forgive you." Forgiveness is not optional but a reflection of God's mercy.

REFLECTION

* Are there unresolved grievances in your marriage that you need to address?
* How can you practice forgiveness in a way that reflects Christ's love?

CHALLENGE

 Identify one area where forgiveness is needed in your relationship. Take the first step by expressing your willingness to forgive or seek forgiveness, and ask God for the grace to move forward in love.

PRAYER

Lord, thank You for forgiving us through Jesus. Help us to reflect Your grace by forgiving each other, even when it's hard. Heal any hurts in our marriage and draw us closer together. In Jesus' name, Amen.

WEEK 52

Leaving a Legacy of Love

*"And now these three remain:
faith, hope, and love.
But the greatest of these is love."*

1 CORINTHIANS 13:13 (NIV)

OBSERVATION

 This verse declares love as the highest virtue, enduring beyond all else. Love is the legacy we leave behind as followers of Christ.

INTERPRETATION

 In marriage, leaving a legacy of love means prioritising love in all you do—toward your spouse, family, and those around you. It's about building a relationship that reflects Christ's love and inspires others to do the same.

CORRELATION

 John 13:34-35 says, "A new command I give you: Love one another. As I have loved you, so you must love one another. By this, everyone will know that you are my disciples." A legacy of love points others to God.

REFLECTION

* What kind of legacy are you building through your marriage?
* How can you make love the foundation of all you do as a couple?

CHALLENGE

 Take time this week to reflect on the past year together. Celebrate the ways your love has grown, and discuss how you want to continue building a legacy of love in the years to come. Write down your shared goals for the future.

PRAYER

Lord, thank You for being the ultimate example of love. Help us to make love the foundation of our marriage, leaving a legacy that glorifies You and inspires others. May our relationship reflect Your goodness and grace. In Jesus' name, Amen.

OTHER BOOKS
BY THE AUTHOR

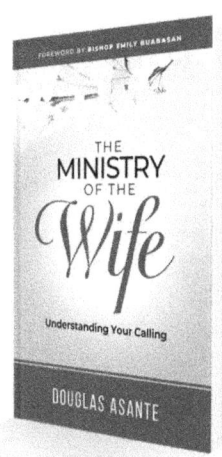  

The Ministry of the Husband
The Ministry of the Wife
365 Daily Devotional

AVAILABLE ON

amazon   amazon kindle

www.dasante.org.uk

www.ingramcontent.com/pod-product-compliance
Lightning Source LLC
Chambersburg PA
CBHW021016090426
42738CB00007B/807